Discovering God

Discovering God

a Personal Bible Study

D. Stuart Briscoe

ZONDERVAN
PUBLISHING HOUSE

OF THE ZONDERVAN CORPORATION
GRAND RAPIDS, MICHIGAN 49506

Discovering God

Copyright © 1975, 1977 by The Zondervan Corporation
Grand Rapids, Michigan

Excerpted from *Getting Into God*

Scripture quotations in the studies are from the *King James Version*. The
memorization list in the appendix to the book employs the *New International
Version, New Testament*, copyright © 1973 by the New York Bible Society
International.

Library of Congress Cataloging in Publication Data

Briscoe, D Stuart.
  Discovering God.

  Originally appeared as pt. 4 of Getting into God.
  1. Bible—Study.   I.   Title.
[BS600.2.B732 1977]   220.6   77-8668

ISBN 0-310-21732-6

Printed in the United States of America

83   84   85   86   87   88 — 10   9   8   7   6

Contents

How to Use This Book

This personal Bible Study is designed to encourage you to dig into the Word of God for yourself. Satan, your relentless enemy, will do everything he can to keep you from finishing even the first lesson. Bible study is work, but it's a work of joy. Paul the apostle charged a young Christian, Timothy, to "study to show thyself approved unto God, a *workman* that needeth not to be ashamed, rightly dividing the word of truth" (2 Tim. 2:15).

This study has been arranged to help you to "rightly divide" the Word of God as to who God is and what He does. From your study you will gain important knowledge that will cause you to mature and be equipped for living and serving (2 Tim. 3:16, 17).

DIG IN

1. Take your study and note the subject given in the major heading.
2. Read each question and look up every reference.

3. The reference will give answers to each question. Write the answer in the space provided.
4. Underline the references neatly in your Bible for further use.
5. Learn by heart the verses suggested in each study. This will enable you to have a few key verses on each subject readily available in your mind for the Holy Spirit's use day by day. The verses are printed in full in the last section of this book.
6. Allow God to speak personally to you through this study of His Word.

PRACTICAL SUGGESTIONS

1. If possible, obtain a file or notebook in which to keep your completed studies.
2. Use a dictionary and look up words you do not understand.

Study No. 1
WHAT IS THE BIBLE?

- Men have been looking for God since time began.
- God wants to be found.
- You can find Him through the Bible, the Word of God.

1. *How does the Bible describe itself?*
   - (1) Luke 8:11 _God's Word is like a seed_
   - (2) Psalm 119:105
     - A. _____
     - B. _____
   - (3) Jeremiah 23:29
     - A. _____
     - B. _____
   - (4) Ephesians 6:17 _____
   - (5) Psalm 19:9, 10
     - A. _____
     - B. _____
   - (6) 1 Peter 2:2 _____

2. *From your answer above, what do you think the Bible should do in your life?*
   - (1) *Seed* _Bring forth fruit (character) in my life_
   - (2) _____
     _____
   - (3) _____
     _____

9

(4) _____

_____

(5) _____

_____

(6) _____

_____

3. *With what subjects does the Bible deal?*
   (1) Philippians 2:16 Life — it is the Word of Life

   (2) Ephesians 1:13 _____

   (3) Acts 13:26 _____

   (4) 2 Corinthians 5:19 _____

   (5) Hebrews 5:13 _____

4. *What did Jesus say about the Word of God?*
   (1) Matthew 4:4 We live by the Word of God

   (2) Matthew 22:29 _____

5. *What ought I to do with the Word of God?*
   (1) Isaiah 34:16 Seek it out and read it

   (2) 2 Timothy 2:15 _____

   (3) Psalm 1:2 _____

   (4) Acts 17:11 _____

   (5) Psalm 119:140 _____

   (6) Luke 24:45 _____

   (7) Psalm 119:9 _____

   (8) Psalm 119:11 _____

   (9) Acts 11:16 _____

   (10) Hebrews 4:2 _____

10

(11) James 1:22 _____

(12) John 8:31 _____

6. *In what way is the Bible of value to me?*

   (1) 2 Timothy 3:15 _____

   (2) John 20:31 — A. _____ B. _____

   (3) 2 Timothy 3:16, It is profitable for A. _____

       B. _____ C. _____ D. _____

       E. _____ F. _____

   (4) Psalm 119:9 _____

   (5) Psalm 119:11 _____

   (6) Psalm 119:130 — A. _____ B. _____

   (7) Romans 15:4 _____

   (8) 1 John 5:13 _____

   (9) 1 Peter 2:2 _____

7. *How is it possible to abuse the Word of God?*

   (1) Mark 7:13 _____

   (2) 2 Corinthians 2:17 _____

   (3) 2 Corinthians 4:2 _____

   (4) Titus 2:5 _____

   (5) 1 Peter 2:8 _____

   (6) Revelation 22:18, 19 — A. _____ B. _____

8. *Learn the following verses and references by heart.*

James 1:22; John 20:31; Psalm 119:105
Underline neatly in your Bible all the verses you have studied.

Study No. 2
WHO IS GOD?

- Men have invented many gods.
- But there is only one God.
- He created the universe and man.

1. *This* one *God consists of* three persons *(sometimes called the Trinity)*
   What are the names of the members of the Trinity?
   Matthew 28:19 — A. Father B. _____ C. _____

2. *The members of the Trinity work together.*
   In the beginning God the Father _____
   the heavens and the earth (Gen. 1:1).
   The Spirit of God _____
   (Gen. 1:2) and all things were made _____
   God's Son and _____ Him (Col. 1:16). Jesus
   was _____ by John the Baptist, and
   the spirit of God _____ upon
   Him, and God the Father said, " _____
   _____ "(Mark 1:9-11).

   (1) *What was the relationship between Father and Son?*
       A. Galatians 4:4 The Father sent the Son
       B. John 3:16 _____
       C. John 5:20 _____
       D. John 8:28 _____
       E. John 8:54 _____
       F. John 10:15 _____

13

G. John 10:18 _____

H. John 11:42 _____

*   *   *

A. John 6:57 _____

B. John 11:41 _____

C. John 17:4 — (a) _____

(b) _____

D. Luke 2:49 _____

(2) *What was the relationship between the Father and the Holy Spirit?*

A. Acts 1:4, 5 _____

B. John 14:26 _____

C. 1 John 4:13 _____

(3) *What was the relationship between the Son and the Holy Spirit?*

A. Luke 1:35 _____

B. Luke 4:1 _____

C. Luke 4:18 _____

D. Hebrews 9:14 _____

E. John 14:26 _____

F. John 15:26 _____

G. John 16:14 _____

3. *What is the attitude of the Trinity to the world?*

(1) Father — John 3:16 _____

(2) Son — 1 Tim. 1:15 _____

(3) Spirit — John 16:8 _____

4. *What is the attitude of the world to the Trinity?*
   (1) Father — John 17:25 _____
   (2) Son — John 15:18 _____
   (3) Spirit — John 14:17 _____
5. *What should my attitude be?*
   (1) To Father — John 4:23; Deut. 6:5 _____
   _____
   (2) To Son — John 20:31; Col. 2:6 — A. _____
   B. _____
   (3) To Spirit — Eph. 5:18; Gal. 5:16 _____
6. *What should I not do?*
   (1) Father — Deut. 8:11 _____
   (2) Son — 2 Tim. 1:8 _____
   (3) Spirit — Eph. 4:30; 1 Thess. 5:19 _____
7. *What should my experience be?* 2 Corinthians 13:14
   (1) Father _____
   (2) Son _____
   (3) Spirit _____
8. *Memorize the following verses:*
   John 3:16; Colossians 2:6; 1 Timothy 1:15.

Study No. 3
WHAT IS GOD LIKE?

- God wants us to know He exists.
- But He also wants us to know Him personally.
- We need to know what He is like.

1. *What are the characteristics of God?*
   (1) *His attributes*
       A. Leviticus 19:2 He is Holy _____
       B. John 17:25 _____
       C. 1 John 4:8 _____
       D. 1 Corinthians 1:9 _____
       E. Genesis 21:33 _____
       F. Genesis 17:1 _____
       G. Deuteronomy 4:31 _____
       H. Joshua 3:10 _____
       I. Nehemiah 1:5 — (a) _____
                         (b) _____
       J. Jonah 4:2 _____

              * * * * * *

       A. Romans 15:5 _____
       B. Romans 15:13 _____
       C. Romans 15:33 _____
       D. 2 Corinthians 1:3 _____
   (2) *His autobiography*
       Exodus 34:6 — He says He is:
       A. _____

16

B. _____

C. _____

D. _____

E. _____

(3) *His faithfulness*

   A. 1 John 1:9 _____

   B. 1 Corinthians 10:13 _____

   C. Lamentations 3:22, 23 _____

   D. Hebrews 10:23 _____

   E. 1 Thessalonians 5:24 _____

   F. 2 Thessalonians 3:3 _____

(4) *His ability*

   A. Hebrews 7:25 _____

   B. 2 Timothy 1:12 _____

   C. Jude v. 24 — (a) _____

               (b) _____

   D. Romans 14:4 _____

   E. Ephesians 3:20 _____

   F. Romans 4:21 _____

   G. Acts 20:32 — (a) _____

               (b) _____

   H. Hebrews 11:19 _____

   I. 2 Corinthians 9:8 _____

2. *What about God and man?*

(1) Genesis 1:27 _____

(2) Genesis 6:5 _____

(3) Psalm 26:2 _____

(4) Romans 1:18 _____

(5) Romans 2:16 _____

(6) Romans 5:8 _____

(7) 2 Peter 3:9 — A. _____

B. _____

C. _____

(8) 1 Timothy 2:4 — A. _____

B. _____

(9) Acts 17:30 _____

(10) John 14:23 — A. _____

B. _____

3. *What will God be to me personally?*

(1) Psalm 23:1 _____

(2) Psalm 27:1 _____

(3) Psalm 28:7 _____

(4) Psalm 94:22 — A. _____

B. _____

(5) Psalm 18:2 — A. _____

B. _____

C. _____

D. _____

E. _____

F. _____

G. _____

H. _____

4. *What should I be to Him?*
   (1)   2 Timothy 3:17 _____
   (2)   John 1:12 _____
   (3)   Romans 8:16, 17 — A. _____
                             B. _____
   (4)   Titus 1:1_____
5. *What must my attitude be to Him?*
   (1)   Psalm 116:1 _____
   (2)   Psalm 37:3 _____
   (3)   Psalm 37:4 _____
   (4)   Psalm 37:5 _____
   (5)   Psalm 37:7 — A. _____
                       B. _____
6. *Memorize the following verses:*
   Romans 5:8; 2 Corinthians 9:8; 1 Corinthians
   10:13

Study No. 4
IS JESUS CHRIST GOD?

- God sent Jesus into the world.
- He came to show God in language we understand.
- But how can we know Jesus is God?

1. *Because of the prophecies He fulfilled*
   - (1) *His birth*
     - A. The Old Testament (Gen. 3:15) said He
       would be . . .
       The New Testament (Gal. 4:4) said He
       was . . .

       born of a woman

     - B. Genesis 18:18 said He would be . . .
       Luke 3:33, 34 said He was . . .

     - C. Numbers 24:17 said He would be . . .
       Luke 3:33, 34 said He was . . .

     - D. Genesis 49:10 said He would be . . .
       Luke 3:33, 34 said He was . . .

     - E. Micah 5:2 said He would be . . .
       Matthew 2:1 said He was . . .

     - F. Isaiah 7:14 said He would be . . .
       Luke 1:26-35 said He was . . .

   - (2) *His life*
     - A. The Old Testament (Isa. 9:1, 2) said
       He would . . .

The New Testament (Matt. 4:12-16) said
He was . . .

B. Isaiah 61:1, 2 said He would be . . .
Luke 4:16-21 said He was . . .

C. Psalm 69:9 said He would . . .
John 2:14-17 said He was . . .

D. Isaiah 35:4-6 said He would . . .
Matthew 9:27-35 said He was . . .

E. Zechariah 9:9 said He would . . .
John 12:12-14 said He was . . .

F. Isaiah 53:3 said He would . . .
John 1:11 said He was . . .

---

(3) *In His betrayal and trial*
A. The Old Testament (Psalm 41:9) He
would . . .
The New Testament (Mark 14:10) said
He was . . .

B. Zechariah 11:12 said He would . . .
Matthew 26:15 said He was . . .

C. Psalm 27:12 said He would . . .
Matthew 26:60, 61 said He was . . .

D. Isaiah 53:7 said He would . . .
Matthew 26:62, 63 said He was . . .

_____

E. Isaiah 50:6 said He would . . .
Mark 14:65 said He was . . .

_____

(4) *In His death*
A. Old Testament (Isa. 53:12) said He would . . .
New Testament (Matt. 27:38) said He was . . .

_____

B. Psalm 22:6-8 said He would . . .
Matthew 27:39, 40 said He was . . .

_____

C. Psalm 22:18 said He would . . .
Mark 15:24 said He was . . .

_____

D. Psalm 69:21 said He would . . .
Matthew 27:34 said He was . . .

_____

E. Psalm 34:20 said He would . . .
John 19:31-33 said He was . . .

_____

2. *Because of the claims He made*

(1) Luke 22:69, 70 _____

(2) John 14:7-10 _____

(3) John 8:58 (see Exod. 3:14) _____

(4) Mark 14:61, 62 _____

(5)   John 9:35-38 _____

3. *Because of the miracles He performed*

  (1)   Matt. 4:23, 24 _____

  (2)   John 11:38-44 _____

  (3)   John 6:9-14 _____

  (4)   Mark 5:1-17 _____

4. *Because of the attributes He displayed*

  (1) Omnipresence   Matt 18:20 _____

      (He can be everywhere) John 2:24, 25 _____

  (2) Omniscience   Mark 11:2-4 _____

      (He knew everything) John 4:16-19 _____

  (3) Omnipotence   Matt. 28:18 _____

      (He could do anything) John 19:28 _____

5. *Because of the testimonies He received from:*

  (1)   Father _____ Matt. 17:5

  (2)   Peter _____ Matt. 16:16

  (3)   John _____John 1:1

  (4)   John the Baptist _____John 1:34

  (5)   Paul _____ Acts 9:19, 20

  (6)   Andrew _____John 1:40, 41

  (7)   Nathanael _____John 1:49

  (8)   Samaritan woman _____John 4:29

  (9)   Martha _____ John 11:27

  (10) Centurion _____Mark 15:39

(11) Devils _____ Matt. 8:28, 29

6. *Because of His resurrection He was declared to be the Son of God by the* _____

_____ Rom. 1:3, 4

7. *Memorize the following verses:*

John 10:28; Matthew 17:5; John 1:1

"But these are written, that ye might believe that Jesus is the Christ, the Son of God; and that believing ye might have life through his name" (John 20:31).

Study No. 5
WHY DID CHRIST LIVE?

- God isn't a vague being.
- He is a living reality.
- The life of Christ shows us how real!

1. *Jesus Christ was both God and Man.*

   (1) *What divine characteristics did He display?*

      A. *Divine power*

         a. Matthew 8:26 _____

         b. John 10:18 _____

      B. *Divine knowledge*

         a. Matthew 17:27 _____

         b. Luke 5:4-6 _____

         c. John 6:64 _____

         d. John 19:28 _____

      C. *Divine predictions*

         a. Mark 8:31 _____

         b. Luke 9:22 _____

         c. John 7:33 _____

   (2) *What did He reveal about God?*

      A. 1 Timothy 3:16 _____

      B. 1 John 4:9 _____

      C. John 2:11 _____

      D. 1 John 1:2 _____

      E. John 17:6 _____

(3) *What human characteristics did He display?*

    A. Matthew 26:34 _____

    B. Luke 2:40 _____

    C. Luke 4:2 _____

    D. Luke 8:23 _____

    E. Luke 9:58 _____

    F. John 4:6 _____

(4) *What human limitations did He have?*

    A. John 8:28 _____

    B. John 5:19 _____

    C. John 5:30 _____

(5) *What was the principle of His life?*

    A. John 14:10 _____

    B. John 8:29 _____

    C. John 5:30 _____

(6) *Why did He come into the world?*

    A. 1 Timothy 1:15 _____

    B. John 10:10 _____

    C. John 18:37 _____

    D. John 12:46 _____

    E. Matthew 9:13 _____

    F. Luke 19:10 _____

    G. John 6:38 _____

    H. Galatians 4:5 — (a) _____

                        (b) _____

2. *What effect did His life have on*
   (1) The Devil? — Matt. 4:1-11 _____

   John 14:30 _____

   (2) The disciples? — Luke 5:8 _____

   Mark 6:51 _____

   (3) The people? — Mark 5:42 _____

   John 7:46 _____

   (4) His enemies? — Luke 23:4 _____

   John 7:1 _____

3. *What is the value of His life?*
   (1) *Shows me what God is like*
      A. Colossians 1:15 _____

      B. John 14:9 _____

   (2) *His sinlessness condemns my sinfulness*
      A. 2 Corinthians 5:21 _____

      B. Hebrews 4:15 _____

      C. 1 Peter 2:22 _____

      D. 1 John 3:5 _____

   (3) *Shows how God expects life to be lived*
      A. John 6:57 _____

      B. Explain this in your own words [see questions (4) and (5) above] _____

      _____

      _____

      _____

(4) *His sinless life qualified Him to die for sinners*

    A. Isaiah 53:6 _____

    B. 1 Peter 3:18 _____

4. *Memorize the following verses:*

   1 Timothy 1:15; 1 John 4:9; 1 Peter 3:18

Study No. 6
WHY DID CHRIST DIE?

- God didn't send Christ just to live.
- He sent Him to die.
- You need to understand the meaning of His death.

1. *What is the meaning of Christ's death?*

   Romans 5:8 — "While we were yet sinners, Christ died for us."

   (1) *Christ's death was* violent

   A. *What were His physical sufferings?*

   (a) John 19:1 _____

   (b) John 19:2 _____

   (c) Matthew 26:67 _____

   (d) Isaiah 50:6 _____

   (e) John 19:18 (see also John 20:25) ____

   (f) Read Psalm 22:14-18.

   B. *What were His mental sufferings?*

   (a) Luke 22:44 _____

   (b) Matthew 27:29 _____

   (c) Luke 23:35 _____

   (d) Luke 23:39 _____

   (e) Matthew 26:56 _____

   C. *What were His spiritual sufferings?*

   (a) 2 Corinthians 5:21 _____

   (b) Isaiah 53:6 _____

   (c) Mark 15:34 _____

   (d) Isaiah 53:10 _____

29

(2) *Christ's death was* voluntary

    A. Hebrews 9:14 _____

    B. John 10:17, 18 _____

    C. John 15:13 _____

(3) *Christ's death was* vicarious *(on behalf of others). For whom did Christ die?*

    A. Hebrews 2:9 _____

    B. Romans 5:6 _____

    C. Romans 5:8 _____

    D. 2 Corinthians 5:15 _____

    E. Ephesians 5:25 _____

    F. Galatians 2:20 _____

    G. Romans 14:15 _____

(4) *Christ's death was* victorious. *What did His death accomplish?*

    A. Hebrews 9:26 _____

    B. Revelation 1:5 _____

    C. 1 Peter 3:18 _____

    D. 2 Corinthians 5:21 _____

    E. Galatians 1:4 _____

    F. Ephesians 1:7 — (a) _____

                     (b) _____

    G. Romans 5:10 _____

    H. Hebrews 2:14 _____

    I. 1 John 1:7 _____

2. *What is sin?*

        Romans 14:23 _____

        James 1:14-15 _____

(1) *How is sin committed?*

  A. Proverbs 10:19 _____

  B. Proverbs 14:21 _____

  C. Proverbs 24:9 _____

  D. James 4:17 _____

  E. 1 John 3:4 _____

(2) *Which people commit sin?*

  A. Romans 3:23 _____

  B. 1 Kings 8:46 _____

  C. Ecclesiastes 7:20 _____

(3) *Why do people commit sin?*

  A. Psalm 51:5 _____

  B. Romans 7:14 _____

  C. Romans 7:20 _____

  D. Mark 7:21-23 _____

(4) *What are the results of sin?*

  A. Romans 6:23._____

     (See also 1 Tim. 5:6; Rev. 3:1; Rev. 20:12-14.)

  B. Psalm 66:18 _____

  C. Isaiah 59:2 _____

  D. Romans 1:24 _____

  E. Ephesians 5:5, 6 _____

F.   Revelation 21:27 _____

2 Corinthians 5:21 and 1 Corinthians 15:3 — "Christ died for our sins."

3. *What must be my attitude toward the Cross?*

   (1)   Galatians 6:14 _____

   (2)   Mark 8:34 _____

   (3)   1 Corinthians 1:18 _____

4. *Learn the following verses:*

   Romans 6:23; Romans 5:8; 2 Corinthians 5:15

Study No. 7
IS CHRIST ALIVE NOW?

- God didn't leave Jesus dead;
  That would have been tragedy.
- He raised Him from the dead;
  That is victory!

List the sequence of events:

Luke 23:52, 53 _____

Matthew 28:2 _____

Mark 16:6 _____

HE IS RISEN!

1. *What are the evidences for His resurrection?*

   (1) *What had Jesus predicted?*

   A. Matthew 20:19 _____

   B. John 2:18-21 _____

   C. John 11:25 _____

   (2) *What had the Old Testament prophesied?*

   Psalm 16:10 _____

   (3) *Who saw Him after His resurrection?*

   A. 1 Corinthians 15:5-8

   (a) _____ (d) _____

   (b) _____ (e) _____

   (c) _____ (f) _____

   (4) *What happened to His body?*

   Luke 24:3 _____

33

(5) *What happened to the disciples?*

    A. Compare Matt. 26:71-74 and Acts 2:14

       Before the resurrection, Peter _____

       After the resurrection, Peter _____

    B. Compare John 20:25 and John 20:28

       _____

       _____

    C. Compare Mark 14:50 and Acts 4:33

       _____

       _____

(6) *What did Paul say?*

    A. Acts 22:6, 7 _____

    B. Acts 26:15, 16 _____

2. *What are the results of His resurrection?*

  (1) *Christ*

    A. Romans 1:4 _____

    B. Colossians 1:18 _____

    C. Acts 10:40 _____

    D. Ephesians 1:20, 21 _____

  (2) *Mankind*

    A. Acts 24:15 _____

    B. John 5:28, 29 _____

    C. Daniel 12:2 _____

    D. Romans 14:9 _____

(3) *Christians*

    A. Romans 4:25 _____

    B. Romans 10:9 _____

    C. Romans 5:10 _____

    D. John 14:19 _____

    E. 1 Thessalonians 4:14 _____

    F. 1 Peter 1:3 _____

    G. Romans 8:11 _____

3. *What should be my experience of His resurrection?*

(1) Colossians 2:12 — "Ye are risen with Him . . ." — raised with Him to a new life, sharing His resurrection life.
Therefore I must —

    A. Colossians 3:1 _____

    B. Colossians 3:2 _____

    C. Colossians 3:5 _____

    D. Colossians 3:8 _____

    E. Colossians 3:12 _____

    F. Colossians 3:15 — (a) _____

                     (b) _____

    G. Colossians 3:16 _____

    H. Colossians 3:17 _____

(2) Galatians 2:20 — The Risen Christ lives in me.
Therefore I should —

    A. Philippians 3:10 _____

    B.   Ephesians 1:18, 19 _____

    C.   Galatians 2:8 _____

4. *Learn the following verses:*

    Galatians 2:20; Romans 10:9; Colossians 2:12

Study No. 8
WHO IS THE HOLY SPIRIT?

- God showed Himself generally in creation.
- He revealed Himself particularly in Christ.
- He reveals Himself personally in the Holy Spirit by coming to live with you.

1. *The Holy Spirit is a Person*

  (1) *Which personal acts does He perform?*

    A. John 14:17 _____

    B. John 16:13 _____

      (a) _____

      (b) _____

      (c) _____

      (d) _____

    C. Acts 13:2 _____

    D. Acts 13:4 _____

    E. Romans 8:26 _____

  (2) *Which personal attributes does He display?*

    A. 1 Corinthians 12:11 _____

    B. Romans 8:27 _____

    C. 1 Corinthians 2:13 _____

    D. Romans 15:13 _____

  (3) *How did Christ speak of Him as a Person?*

    A. John 14:16 _____

    B. John 14:17

      (a) _____

      (b) _____

      (c) _____

      (d) _____

(4) *How is it possible to treat Him as a Person?*

  A. Acts 5:3 _____

  B. Acts 5:9 _____

  C. Acts 7:51 _____

  D. Ephesians 4:30 _____

  E. Hebrews 10:29 _____

2. *The Holy Spirit is God*

(1) *By which divine titles is He called?*

  A. Genesis 6:3 _____

  B. 2 Chronicles 15:1 _____

  C. Isaiah 11:2 _____

  D. Isaiah 61:1 _____

  E. Matthew 10:20 _____

  F. Romans 8:9 _____

  G. Galatians 4:6 _____

(2) *Which divine attributes does He display?*

  A. Hebrews 9:14 _____

  B. 1 John 5:6 _____

  C. 1 Thessalonians 4:8 _____

  D. Psalm 139:7-10 _____

  E. 1 Corinthians 2:10 _____

(3) *Which divine tasks does He perform?*

    A. Job 26:13 _____

    B. Matthew 12:28 _____

    C. John 3:5 _____

(4) *In which great events did He participate?*

    A. Genesis 1:2 _____

    B. Matthew 1:18-20 _____

    C. Luke 4:1 _____

    D. Hebrews 9:14 _____

    E. Romans 8:11 _____

    F. 2 Peter 1:21 _____

3. *What are the Holy Spirit's qualities?*

    A. Romans 1:4 _____

    B. Isaiah 11:2 — (a) _____

                      (b) _____

                        (c) _____

                        (d) _____

                        (e) _____

                        (f) _____

    C. Zechariah 12:10 _____

    D. John 14:17 _____

    E. Romans 8:2 _____

    F. Romans 8:15 _____

    G. 2 Corinthians 4:13 _____

    H. 2 Timothy 1:7 — (a) _____

(b) _____

(c) _____

I. Hebrews 10:29 _____

J. 1 Peter 4:14 _____

K. Isaiah 4:4 — (a) _____

(b) _____

4. *What should be my experience of the Holy Spirit?*

I must be _____ of the Spirit (John 3:8)
that I might _____ in the Spirit (Gal 5:25). If I
_____ in the Spirit (Gal. 5:25) day by day, I will
not _____ (Gal. 5:16).
If I refuse to yield to the Spirit living with-
in me, I will _____
the Spirit (1 Thess. 5:19) and _____
_____ the Spirit (Eph. 4:30). I must be
continually _____ with the Spirit
(Eph. 5:18) now that I have become an _____
_____ of _____ _____
through the Spirit (Eph. 2:22). As I am _____
by the Spirit (Romans 8:14) I will be _____
by the Spirit (Eph. 3:16), and He shall _____

_____

(John 14:26) and I will be filled with _____
and _____ through the power of
the Holy Spirit (Romans 15:13).

5. *Learn the following verses:*

John 14:17; Romans 8:26; 1 Peter 4:14

"Study to shew thyself approved unto God, a workman that needeth not to be ashamed, rightly dividing the word of truth."

— 2 Timothy 2:15

Verses to Memorize

Study No. 1

Do not merely listen to the word, and so deceive yourselves. Do what it says.

— James 1:22

But these are written that you may believe that Jesus is the Christ, the Son of God, and that by believing you may have life in his name.

— John 20:31

Thy word is a lamp unto my feet, and a light unto my path.

— Psalm 119:105 KJV

Study No. 2

For God so loved the world that he gave his one and only Son, that whoever believes in him shall not perish but have everlasting life.

— John 3:16

So then, just as you received Christ Jesus as Lord, continue to live in him.

— Colossians 2:6

Here is a trustworthy saying that deserves full acceptance: Christ Jesus came into the world to save sinners — of whom I am the worst.

— 1 Timothy 1:15

But God demonstrates his own love for us in this: While we were still sinners, Christ died for us.

— *Romans 5:8*

And God is able to make all grace abound to you, so that in all things at all times, having all that you need, you will abound in every good work.

— *2 Corinthians 9:8*

No temptation has seized you except what is common to man. And God is faithful; he will not let you be tempted beyond what you can bear. But when you are tempted, he will also provide a way out so that you can stand up under it.

— *1 Corinthians 10:13*

Study No. 4

I give them eternal life, and they shall never perish; no one can snatch them out of my hand.

— *John 10:28*

While he was still speaking, a bright cloud enveloped them, and a voice from the cloud said, "This is my Son, whom I love; with him I am well-pleased. Listen to him!

— *Matthew 17:5*

In the beginning was the Word, and the Word was with God, and the Word was God.

— *John 1:1*

Study No. 5

This is how God showed his love among us: He sent his one and only Son into the world that we might live through him.

— *1 John 4:9*

For Christ died for your sins once for all, the righteous for the unrighteous, to bring you to God. He was put to death in the body but made alive by the Spirit.

— *1 Peter 3:18*

Study No. 6

For the wages of sin is death, but the gift of God is eternal life through Christ Jesus our Lord.

— *Romans 6:23*

And he died for all that those who live should no longer live for themselves, but for him who died for them and was raised again.

— *2 Corinthians 5:15*

Study No. 7

I have been crucified with Christ and I no longer live, but Christ lives in me. The life I live in the body, I live by faith in the Son of God, who loved me and gave himself for me.

— *Galatians 2:20*

If you confess with your mouth, "Jesus is Lord," and believe in your heart that God raised him from the dead, you will be saved.

— *Romans 10:9*

In baptism you were buried with him and raised with him through your faith in the power of God, who raised him from the dead.

— *Colossians 2:12*

Study No. 8

. . . The Spirit of truth, to be with you forever. The world cannot accept this Counselor, because it neither sees him nor knows him. But you know him, for he lives with you and will be in you.

— *John 14:17*

In the same way, the Spirit helps us in our weakness. We do not know how we ought to pray, but the Spirit himself intercedes for us with groans that words cannot express.

— *Romans 8:26*

If you are insulted because of the name of Christ, you are blessed, for the Spirit of glory and of God rests on you.

— *1 Peter 4:14*

Notes

Notes

Notes